# Zoomorphic

Poems by

Emily Wharton

ISBN: 978-0-9963812-0-8

# Contents

# Acknowledgements

The title "The Fireflies Part The Air With Their Two Hands" was taken from lines in <u>She Says</u> by Venus Khoury-Ghata.

The poem " Read these poems and become a winged creature" appeared in the Backwards City Review.

Many thanks to Paul Wharton for his amazing cover design. I would also like to thank Deborah Keenan, Jim Moore, and all the faculty of the Hamline University MFA program for their wisdom and guidance.

For Shawn, Always.

## Read these poems and become a
### winged creature

Not an eagle or hawk, though,
more likely a chicken.
I'm afraid you'll stay close to the earth
pecking, hopping, scratching, staring
at the dirt. The dirt will be your horizon.
You'll have a grape sized brain and the patterns
of your penned world—your own tracks and
    droppings—
will absorb you all your pre-processing days.
But this is not what I should tell you. I should
    inspire,
uplift, be part of the solution.
but I am as insoluble as mercury-
a liquid ball rolled, shattered, reformed.
I would make you a duck—a city lake duck--
summering among manicured weeds
and graceful on glossy water,
but you would form gangs that barricade
the walking path, bobbing and hissing
until I threw bread. I have no bread to throw--
nothing in my pockets but paper.
Only goats eat paper, and goats have no wings,
vestigial or otherwise.

## Zoomorphic

The walls haven't fallen in on us.
The monotony of monogamy has yet to do us in.
But that doesn't mean we won't still stumble
harnessed to each other and a sled loaded
with everyday glasses and extra bed sheets.
Yet I would pull anything
to feel the solid heat of you,
drag all of it into the wilderness pretending
the tracks we trace belonged to creatures
not eaten or beaten or frozen
just beyond the next ridge.
Because I'm a lemming? Because I'm a cow?
Because I can't stand alone in the short grass
without shaking? Keep pulling, my love.
Our hooves will cut into the snow pack
without question or deliberation.
We shall molt and never speak
of our old skins again. We can feed
on our neighbors, our placentas, our drapery.
We will grow fit and survive
or be the last to die,
burrowed in for the winter,
muzzle to muzzle,
flank to flank.

The fireflies part the air with
   their two hands

because their mother's told them: always
use two hands—or was it always
wash both hands?

Fireflies are always trying
to get away with something,
just because they are beautiful,
just because they beat Edison
by a million years.

But my mother pulls off their bulbs
to make them into rings.
She won't stop making rings
until she has one for each finger
of both of her two hands.

## Rabid Skunk Loose In Town

We watch Main Street caramelize
arguing if it bit one of us,
would they shoot us like Old Yeller?

My mom says of course not
we'd get forty shots
with a four inch needle
right in the gut.

She gives us apples with salt.
The afternoon slips into a coma.

Beasel swears he'll kill it,
says he has a bee bee gun
but won't ride home and get it.

You throw your core in the middle of the sidewalk
and won't pick it up no matter how much I beg.

You want to see it up close.
You know you can make it come to you.

## Mamma says

stay to the left, there's a pigeon.
It flutters like a tub toy
but doesn't lift two inches.
Mamma says it's going to die.
She says something dies every day,
but most days we don't see it
because it gets cleaned up
before we get there.
Mamma says don't touch,
but its whole body
feels as light as its wings.

## The Northbound Geese of November

I want to hope them a fate
other than frozen starvation,
but Nature is a bad mother.
If the universe had a child welfare office,
Nature would have a case worker at her door,
even though she's more compassionate
than the cat people discovered
with thirty-seven felines pissing
on every inch of a studio apartment.
Nature holds no creature captive,
not even for its own protection.

# Falling

One second, I'm on the ladder pulling
an aluminum blade full of slush
toward me and the gutter,
the next second, I'm seeing only sky--
a foggy cirrus sheet, but bright,
backlit by a thawing sun.
I landed on my back, feet hooking
the rungs of the ladder, I stood
quickly so that I knew that I could
and picked up my hat at the edge
of the patio. Mostly then I said "fuck"
over and over as I walked around
the ladder like it was a whale skeleton
washed ashore with a human skeleton
inside the arch of its ribs. I looked up
at the rake resting on the roof
it's handle dangling at a reachable height
like it's saying, "I dare you to fall in love
with this crazy goddamn luck."
but it was too late, I already had.

## Woman With Cramps Pushing
### Snow Blower

She sets her jaw, focuses the ache of her uterus,
and engages her beefy thighs--powering and
   willing
the shaking beast upright and ahead
into the snowdrift of history--
transfiguring it into a spray
of glittering projectiles,
arcing it into the sun,
clearing one smooth path
through the obstinacy of winter.
She is alone inside the bawl of the Engine.
She smells like gasoline and wet cotton.
She has so many kinds of hope--
though, as you might have guessed,
under her stocking cap
she wears a wig of snakes.

## Snakes & Babies

For centuries it was assumed that Cleopatra used
    an asp
in her suicide, but now those who test such
    theories
have decided it was a cobra.

Thirty years ago, doctors thought babies should
    never
sleep on their backs, but now doctors say not to
    put infants
to bed on their stomachs.

But it has always been held in common truth
that you should never put
a snake in a baby's bed;

Unless you are a mother snake and you live in a
    storybook world
where your baby would sleep in a crib
rather than a hole in the side of a hill.

But even in that case, you could never lay your
    snake baby
and a human baby side by side and go to the
    kitchen
to snap beans and gossip.

You wouldn't have a second thought, but the
    human mother
will decide it might be better if her little darling
rested in the playpen instead.

And what can you do? There's all that history.
Do you get mad, take your child

and slither home in a huff?--

or just say, "You know, Junior does
    have a bit of a cold."
and go put on the coffee?

# Following Birds

"From the foliage a whistling – people or birds?"
– Tomas Transtromer, Lamento

In Germany, the Public Radio reports,
One politician wants to make audible traffic signals
Sound like birds instead of a monotonic
Tick, tick, tick.
Another politician worries
That blind people will get confused
And follow live birds.

Can you imagine?
A hoard of blind people
Chasing a finch!

No, you can't imagine
A hoard of blind people at all.
You know one blind man
And he is lost–
Head down, eyes shaded
Careening toward all manner of obstacle.

Now your day is sidetracked–
You have to run across the street
To save him from that tree–
And he doesn't even remember you from last
    week!
"You must be thinking of someone else" he says.
"Really, I'm fine, I don't need your help,
but thanks anyway."  Can you imagine!

You walk on to the bank noting
How exquisitely red the red
Sections of that Amoco sign look
In this low October sun

17

Humming to yourself
I once was lost
But now I'm found...

# Odysseus on the 21A

Odysseus would never ride the 21A
There are a lot of reasons.
Its not sleek nor trim nor fast.
It's a giant tin of international coffee
with four wheels and a diesel engine
and even late at night it will stop at every corner
to pick someone up or let someone off.
The sirens  he would hear
would not entrance him.
Odysseus couldn't command the 21A.
He can't tell the driver to put his back in the oars.
He couldn't even tell the loud fuck
lying  like a walrus  across the back bench
to shut the hell up or he'll run him through
with a bronze tipped spear.
No driver will let you board carrying a bronze
    tipped spear
They won't even let you on with an unwrapped
    sandwich.
And when he and the walrus get off the bus
six of the walrus' friends
will appear out of nowhere to kick Odysseus' ass
all the way back to Ithaca or Edina
or whatever suburb he came from.

## Gloaming

In a matter of years, we will be gone
into the machine or the dirt,
the circuit or the idea of the circuit.
It is only a matter of years,
yet I have no urge to fight, no instinct to flee,
just a vague sense that I should find my way into
    the woods.
I hug my dog and she looks at me
as if to say: "Let's fetch
the rubber football then
go inside and have dinner."
The football has one end chewed off
and mud on the inside walls, but she still brings it
and will keep bringing it until there is nothing left.
The sun finishes its descent.
I go inside and fix dinner.
Tomorrow we will do all this again
unless it rains.

## Groundhog's Day

the reason I love this Movie
is because eventually the Cycle
is broken and Bill Murray wakes up
to February 3rd because he has mastered
the lesson of February 2nd--which is pure
and unfettered Love for Andy McDowell.

there is so much released in the Moment
Sisyphus' Rock rolls over the Summit
and drops into the Space too holy for Imagining.
it is Orgasm unbounded by the Body.

but you say it's stupid
and takes too long. You refuse
to buy into the Conceit. as a Scientist
you know there is no great Power out there
forcing us to get Anything right--we can
keep slipping on the Entrails of our Fuck-Ups
into Infinity without a statistically significant
Hint of Disapproval

don't get me wrong, i agree in Theory,
but the aching Implausibility of this perpetual Re-
     Do
forces me to watch this Movie
over and over and over again.

# The Pitch

The count: 3 & 2. Full.
On the next pitch, the game turns
unless the batter fouls one off.
What if he fouled
pitch after pitch forever?
Would the world stop?
Is that the eternal present?
Pretend for a moment
that the batter never hits
one just inside the line.
Pretend the pitcher can't find
some extra mustard for his sinker?
What would we do?
Would we stare hunched
like old ladies at nickel slots?
Or would we turn off the TV
and make love right there on the sofa--
lusty and free in the statistical void?
High school physics teaches us
the universe is a Rube Goldberg device--
the pool ball rolling
down the ramp falling
into the bucket dropping
the lever that lifts the cage
and sets the owl free to eat
the mosquito careening
toward the batters ear.
Yes! another tip
rolling to the dugout--
and the game goes further
into the already dark night.

# Trying To Write a Tony Hoagland Poem

I should start with the woman on the bus
the one on the left side of the aisle talking
of the neighbors who have died or gotten married
with the man on the right--who is giving a poor
    performance
of someone who gives a rat's ass. I should avoid
    the mundane
details of coat and hair that I would use to speak
    many
divergent statistics. Instead I should paraphrase
    dialog
then say something smart about how deeply she
    longs for community
and how I want to cry for her.
I think of her with that anxious
sadness I feel every time I realize
too late someone had wanted to be my friend--
made a gesture they thought overt and I
went off to be alone. Somewhere along
the way I need to find a plant or animal
to do something pointless and shocking.
It needs to be an act unique enough
to make the jaded third year grad students
unclamp the pen between their teeth.
This is the hardest part.
They have nerves as waxen and tangled
as the wires behind their computers.
Finally I need to end on the same bus
but be sitting somewhere else--
perhaps in the driver's seat
with a commanding view
of traffic's limitless semiology,
my own ordinary failure,
and the man in the butterfly wings

sprinting to reach the stop
before I pass him by.

## When you discover you will never be Elizabeth Bishop

it will be a relief. You'll get a decent night's sleep,
but then the long term effects will creep over you
    like river fog
or just smack you like Cher smacked that guy in
    Moonstruck.
You'll be walking down the street in your
    hometown
with stripped screws and adjectives jangling in
    your pocket
and five different species of bird you don't know
    the names of
will burst out of a tree you don't recognize
and you'll double over with longing to see the
    world –
the world behind this one – the world you could
    love.

## What is the Most Dangerous Animal in the World?

is the trivia question
on the drive- time radio.
The host says it's a housefly
because of all the bacteria
it transports from sandwich to sandwich.
I had guessed a human
because of all the bombs it transports
from continent to continent.
But we can't think of ourselves
as animals. If we are animals
we've been acting
absurd all day—putting on pants,
taking notes in the meeting,
If we are really animals, we should know
how to lick our wounds
unapologetically in plain sight.
If we were animals, we could find
our way home
cross-country
and as the crow flies.

# On This Day In History

It is the day Amelia Earhart disappeared
and the day Hemingway put a bullet through his
    brain,
yet it was clear like bottled water
and regular as the commuter train
until dusk when the neighborhood opened fire
with M80s and bottle rockets
and my 20 pound Shetland sheepdog
crawled into my lap and tucked
her whole head under my arm.
The three month old puppy
stared at her with head cocked
but she is shameless in her need for comfort.
She stands on my lap, puts one paw on each
    shoulder
and presses her cheek next to mine--
just as she'd seen you do
when you were shaking.
So I stroke her fur, say, "It's OK, baby"
and carry her to bed
where she falls asleep
and I lie awake
on your side of the bed
listening for the end of the world
or the dishwasher's last cycle.
Below me a storage closet full
of suitcases and textbooks waits,
paint and rollers wait, chisels and wooden blocks
    wait.
I wake to thunder and gray rain
behind closed blinds.
I let go of your pillow, dish out kibble,
and make coffee.
It is Franz Kafka's birthday.

and the day Washington surrendered
Fort Necessity.

# Telling people that your dog died

There's this moment, after you've said everything about how it happened and how the other dog is managing and how you are trying to get through, where the person you are talking to has run out of questions and said I'm sorry four times and you just stand there. You know its time to change the subject. You know you have to ask how the new job's going or if Peyton Manning will decide to retire. But you hold off for a few seconds thinking you might actually walk away. You could do it without causing offense. Grieving people are allowed a certain measure of rudeness. But there will have to be, at some time, a point of re-engagement. The black veil will tatter to transparency. Sure, she was a dog, but she never said anything behind your back. She never walked away while tears were on your cheeks. So you put one word in front of the other.  Of course you are standing and not sitting. If you sat down, you would stop listening. You'd think about people fleeing the great fire of Chicago with their dogs in their arms. Then you would see your dog in that post-surgical kennel with her mouth fallen open. The image won't have any logical connection to the story, but you will feel certain that it does.

## Through the Valley

there is fog out every window and I want to  sing
something simple about how fog is beautiful  or
    fog is ugly,
but the fog on the pine trees is beautiful  and the
    fog on the yield signs is ugly
and all of it will—as they say--burn off by ten.
I want to watch fog burn, really burn slow like
    hardwood,
smolder like Cinemax After Dark.
I'd love to taste it, hoard heaps of it in the cave of
    my mouth.
But we are moving through, just rolling through.
This isn't a bad highway, just a recurring dream,
déjà vu all over and over again.
The same hill rising around the same bend
until The fog on the yield signs has gathered
    meaning.
The dragon in my mouth will spend all day indoors
    and unemployed;
hungry, dry and dreamless.

# Close to Happy

1.
It's snot-freezing-on-the-inner-rims- of-your-
    nostrils cold.
It's cold that eats itself
and shits out more cold.
"But the light is coming back, so I can have faith."
the woman at the bus stop says.
"Listen there is a cardinal."

2.
My mother's daughter cannot open
a new bottle of wine for a solitary evening;
even if Oprah thinks she should pamper herself.
Not that she doesn't deserve it,
but that she deserves something else
something ten or twenty years
down the road, or in the next life

3.
The Navy blasted the spy satellite
into manageable toxic pieces
that will incinerate on re-entry
"harmlessly."

4.
The cardinal doesn't have faith.
He is faith.

5.
The flame that fired my ambition
now smolders in my connective tissue.
"How would you rate the pain,  on a scale of 1 to
    10?"
I can't process in decimal.

Some days it is cardinal red smeared with
    cigarette ash.
Others it is the smell of shriveled oranges and
    sulfur.

6.
I am employee of the month.
I have root access.
I can swim the data stream.
I mistake the cardinal for a ringtone.

7.
The Moment of Truth
"For $100,000, the question is
Do you feel you are wasting your life?"

8.
The cardinal doesn't know
that he is faith,
nor does he care.

9.
Last week a man died in an S&M parlor
the dominatrix left him there to anticipate
and instead he asphyxiated.
The line between as much as one can take
and too much isn't just thin,
it's wavy like the breathing
of the man in the bus seat behind me.
He releases a little sing-song "yes, yes, yes,"
into the commuter silence.

# Mass of the Resurrection

I'm not going to mock anything—not the prayers
nor the robes, not the kneeling nor the little pink
    priest
who can't remember if he's talking about Jesus or
    the deceased.
If she loved this, I can too for one day.
I cry through Amazing Grace and On Eagle's Wings
and my cheek muscles throb
from the effort of holding it to a level
suitable for a new subdivision in North Morehead.
During the middle ages, incense was used
to cover the stench of the unembalmed corpse,
but now it floats through a sea of perfumes
body washes, deodorants,
and grief--which nothing covers adequately.
I try to decide
whether the sky provides background
for the cross timbers or the cross divides
the porthole of sky.
Either way it's Easter egg
bleaching to robin's egg
and the skylight has sent
a gold bar of sun inching
from the pulpit to the casket
that will not arrive before
the slow sigh of the benediction
and the hotdish, buttered bread, pickles,
and bars--three kinds of bars--
and women in freshly ironed dresses
who glide from table to table
offering us more of everything.